Old SALTCOATS

by

R. & M. McSherry

"Saltcoats fur ever"!

© Copyright 1995 R. & M. McSherry
First Published in the United Kingdom, 1995
By Richard Stenlake, Ochiltree Sawmill, The Lade, Ochiltree, Ayrshire KA18 2NX
Telephone: 01290 700266

ISBN 1-872074-57-X

The Burgh of Saltcoats seal depicts four symbols associated with the town and its heritage. A lymphad, sail furled and oars in action, represents Saltcoats' one time shipping and shipbuilding activities. The building in the top right corner is a salt pan. A fish represents the former fishing industry, and the three amulets are taken from the coat of arms of the Earls of Eglinton and Winton, whose ancestor Hugh, first Earl of Eglinton was granted permission to erect Saltcoats to a Burgh of Barony in 1528. The motto reads 'By Sea and Land'.

INTRODUCTION

Saltcoats derives its name from the ancient practice of boiling sea water to extract salt, a practice which its inhabitants once carried out in their beachside 'cots' (houses). The fuel needed for salt production was provided by locally mined coal, and as the town's fishing industry prospered, demand for salt, used to cure fish, steadily increased. These industries - salt production, coal mining, and fishing - along with local handloom weaving, provided the basis for Saltcoats' expansion and prosperity.

A crumbling stone (no longer extant) in a churchyard neighbouring Kilwinning Abbey is reported to have mentioned 'Hew Fergus, curate of Ye Chappel Brae Saut-Cottes' and borne the date 1272. Whatever the true date of its foundation, Saltcoats was well established by 1528, when a charter was granted to Hugh, Earl of Eglinton allowing the settlement to become a Burgh of Barony. Feuding between the Cunninghames of Glencairn and the Montgomeries of Eglinton led to violence and recrimination in Saltcoats, with the unrest coming to a head in 1526. Edward Cunninghame, Lord Glencairn, was murdered by the Montgomeries and their allies, and in revenge, Glencairn's eldest son and his supporters raided Montgomerie territory burning the castle and lands, and leaving tenants destitute and starving. Restoration of the peace was due in part to the intervention of James V, who entered the fray on behalf of the Earl of Eglinton.

But Saltcoats became a Burgh of the Barony in 1528, at which time stability and harmony was restored. The town's inhabitants received trading rights and were also permitted to hold two annual fairs, both of which led to social and economic improvements. Local industry flourished, aided by the construction of a harbour which was begun in 1684 and completed six years later. Busy with both local and foreign shipping trade, this was expanded with the addition of an outer pier around 1800, while a two mile stretch of canal, constructed in 1772, connected it with local coal fields. Meanwhile, two large salt pans were created to cope with the burgeoning salt trade, several shipbuilding yards were active, and Saltcoats' population of handloom weavers numbered around five hundred.

Around the turn of the twentieth century new manufacturing processes led to the decline of salt panning in Saltcoats, and this had a knock-on effect on the local coal industry, which supplied the fuel necessary for salt extraction. However, as traditional local industries fell into decline, Saltcoats benefitted from its increasing popularity as a holiday destination. The addition of esplanades to both the east and west shores constituted significant improvements to the seafront, and during the thirties the old bathing pond was reconstructed. As the largest tidal pool in Scotland, this proved extremely popular, with both locals and visitors keeping the turnstiles clicking, especially during the summer months. Minstrels, pierrots, and other travelling entertainers provided amusement for the holiday-makers, while bands frequently performed at the Melbourne Park bandstand. From the twenties to the fifties, many well known stage entertainers played at the Beach Pavilion during the summer 'season'. But as foreign travel became increasingly popular and affordable, Saltcoats' holiday trade declined. The bathing pool closed, and after being used by the shellfish industry for a time it was finally demolished in 1985.

Saltcoats ceased to exist as an independent burgh in 1975, when it was integrated within Cunninghame District Council. Enormous changes have been made to the town over the centuries, and several of the places illustrated in this book have long since vanished. Many of Saltcoats' landmarks owe their memory to the postcard producers, who so avidly recorded the face of Britain at the turn of the century.

Quay Street, Saltcoats.

Quay Street, circa 1905, looking towards Countess Street and the town hall steeple. Better known to the locals as the 'Pan Brae', this was home to many of the town's fishing and seafaring folk including the legendary Betsy Miller, the first female captain of a British ship mentioned in the British Register of Tonnage. These houses have long since been demolished, although a plaque on one of the modern flats records where Betsy Miller once lived.

A busy scene at the junction of Ardrossan and Caledonia Roads. Today there is a roundabout here with five exits from it. Note the lean-to houses beside what was Bankside House.

Saltcoats was a popular destination with Glasgwegians during the annual Glasgow Fair, as the crowds in this shot of Saltcoats station show. Many of the travellers are wearing their finest outfits for the occasion. The station master's house, ticket office and waiting room are on the right.

This accident occurred at Saltcoats station on 18th August 1906, injuring over eighty people. Another serious crash took place in 1939 when a passenger train came off the rails and plunged into the gardens of the National Miners Home at Canal Street. Miners from the home helped to release the driver and fireman from the wreckage, although both later died, along with two passengers. Many more people were seriously injured.

MOTOR-BOATING AT SALTCOATS.

49982

Activities for holidaymakers in Saltcoats were many and varied, and during the twenties motorboat trips could be had at both the east and west bays. Here, the west bay jetty stretches out from the beach, allowing for the rise and fall of the tide.

The east bay motorboats were stationed at Saltcoats harbour. In this turn of the century view, tourists can be seen descending the wooden ladders that were used to access the boats - not such a simple operation when the sea was rougher! Note the fishing nets hanging out to dry on the sea wall.

Bathing Station, Saltcoats

Saltcoats Bathing Station, pictured in 1910, was situated on a rocky spot at Winton Circus. It developed in stages, starting off as a small pool with changing facilities, and was reconstructed by the Burgh as a large tidal pool in 1933. For many years the tidal pool, with its accompanying tearoom, was a popular meeting place. There was a flourishing swimming club, and the bathing station was also home to the first Life Guards section in the West of Scotland. The site was redeveloped in 1989 and is now a landscaped area. Today, swimmers can enjoy greater comfort at Harvies heated indoor pool, Auchenharvie.

In the fifties, midnight swimming took place during the summer, providing the weather was suitable.

Saltcoats catered for every taste, and amongst the acts that performed in the town were Harry Kemp's, whose name was synonymous with entertainment in Clyde resorts from Dunoon to Troon. Kemp's motto was short and to the point: 'if its H.K. its O.K!', and many well known entertainers, such as Dave Willis, Tommy Morgan and the Houston Sisters started their career with him. The 'Regal Revels', pictured here, performed in Saltcoats in 1932.

Right: The Ardrossan and Saltcoats Players club was founded in 1908. Their 1928 performance of Sir James Barrie's one act play, 'The Old Lady Shows her Medals', won acclaim in both Britain and America, where it received the coveted David Belasco Trophy. Miss Isabel Jamieson, who played the old lady, and Jack Lambert, the young soldier are pictured here.

Casino Picture House, Hamilton Street, Saltcoats

The Casino Picture House only showed silent films, and with the advent of 'talkies' in 1929 it was demolished. The Regal, built on the same site, opened its doors in 1931 with a screening of the French Foreign Legion story, 'Beau Ideal', a sequel to 'Beau Geste'. Nowadays, the Regal operates as the Metropolis nightclub.

Sydney Street, Saltcoats.

Sydney Street looking north towards Eglinton Street, pictured around the turn of the century. This was a popular street for holiday accomodation, with good access to both the beaches and the town.

14

Ardrossan Road looking east, at the Galloway Burn Bridge with the old iron footbridge leading to Stanley Road in the background. The road has been widened considerably since this turn of the century picture.

Windmill Street as pictured here is unrecognisable today. The thatched fishermen's cottages on the right were demolished in the forties during road improvements, and the buildings on the left have been replaced by Eglinton Court.

Caledonia Road near the junction with Argyll Road circa 1905. Three of the boys in the postcard are carrying delivery baskets from local shops. During World War II this area of the road was the site of a large emergency water tank, but is now a raised triangular shaped garden.

Raise Street looking north. During the eighteenth and nineteenth centuries this area of town was home to the Salt-coats weavers, and was known locally as weaverland. Many of the town's worthies lived here too, although it must have been a noisy area, with several hundred hand looms operating. The weavers were proud of their trade, and leading figures in the industry made themselves recognisable by wearing 'Lum Hats'. They even had their own Political Trade Parliament, roughly equivalent to an early trade union. Mechanical progress and the advent of large factories gradually caused a decline in weaving in Saltcoats, and all the buildings on this postcard have now been demolished.

Hamilton Street, Saltcoats

Hamilton Street looking west. On the right is the E.U. Congregational Church. Built in 1863 and closed for worship in 1991, the building is currently used as a furniture store. Most of the buildings on the church side of the street have been demolished and replaced with shops, and many of the houses on the other side have been converted for use as shops.

Saltcoats, On the Esplanade.

Saltcoats Esplanade on a summers day around the turn of the century. The beach attracted entertainers such as 'The Pierrots', and was often the venue for religious orators too. There were sand castle building competitions for the children, as well as the occasional Punch and Judy show.

20

Hampson's Pierrots Summer Outdoor Entertainers with their stage and hut erected outside the bathing station circa 1920. It was obviously standing room only for this performance! Note the early motorcycle on this card. Number-plates such as the one visible here are now avidly sought by collectors.

Rough Sea at East Beach, Saltcoats.

The canal from Auchenharvie coal pits terminated at Saltcoats' east beach, and materials were then transported along the seafront to the harbour by horse rail. This picture was taken before the promenade was built, and shows the chimneys of the Stevenston Iron Foundries in the distance. The railway line runs parallel to the shore, and high seas often cause disruption to the service, especially now that it has been electrified.

Saltcoats from the Harbour.

A 1904 view of the harbour showing the old stone quay and the Braes before the sea wall was built. Note the fisherwomen on the quay.

This 1910 picture, taken from the Bay, shows how much reclamation work needed to be carried out before the construction of the sea wall and the area known as the Braes could go ahead. Some buildings on Dockhead Street are still standing, but all the ones around the Bay have long since been demolished. Modern flats were built on the site in the sixties.

Canal Street, Saltcoats

Canal street, named, surprisingly, after the canal that was constructed nearby in 1772! It was the first commercial transport canal in Scotland and was used by horse drawn barges which hauled coal from the Auchenharvie mines to the harbour. From there most of it was shipped to Ireland.

Saltcoats Quater Centenary Celebrations, 1928

R. V. Br   Pho

A popular event in the Saltcoats' calendar was the crowning of the 'Sea Queen', a tradition started by Provost W.D. Kerr in 1928 to mark the Saltcoats' Quater Centenary Celebrations (1528-1928). The Queen and her attendants were selected in rotation from the four local schools: Ardrossan Academy, Saltcoats Public, St. Mary's and Kyleshill; the only stipulation being that pupils taking part had to be resident in Saltcoats. The ceremony ceased after 1935, although it was revived during the fifties, continuing until 1963.

R. V. Brown, Photo

The first Queen of the Sea was Netta Duff of Ardrossan Academy, pictured here with her attendants in 1928.

EMPIRE DAY AT SALTCOATS SCHOOL – "SALUTING THE FLAG"

The first Empire Day celebrations to be held at Saltcoats' Public School in 1909. Immediately behind the Boy Scout taking the salute is Mr Alexander Watters, the school janitor. The houses in the background are in Caledonia Road Brae.

Sports Day at Saltcoats Public School circa 1900 being held on what is now the site of St Cuthbert's South Beach Church. The wooden hoops used in the race were propelled by the competitors using a short wooden stick.

Melbourne Park, on the West Shore. The two putting greens and bandstand were later additions to the park, although both the original bandstand and its successor have long since gone. In this early view, an ice-cream vendor poses proudly by his stall.

At the Bandstand, Saltcoats.

As well as the burgh band, the town council invited brass and silver bands from other parts of Ayrshire to come and play at the bandstand in Melbourne Park, and the performances were very popular with visitors and townspeople alike. The old Westfield Hotel can be seen in the right of the picture. This has now been demolished and replaced by the Westfield Court flats.

Hamilton Street as viewed from Caledonia Road Brae about 1904. The building facing the camera was the local jail behind which was the Gaelic Church, later to become the North Parish Church. Today the War Memorial and Safeway's occupy this site

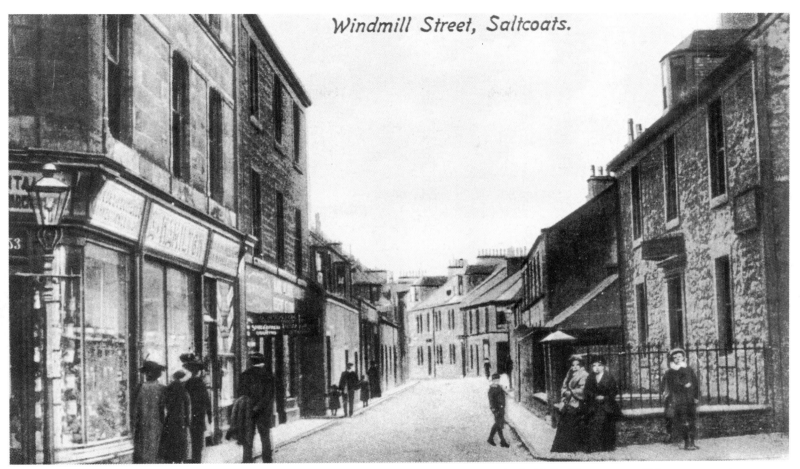

Windmill Street, Saltcoats.

All the houses on the right of Windmill Street have long since been demolished. Holly House, a well known guest residence, is the large building on the right, and behind A. Hamilton's general store (with the advert for State Express cigarettes outside) is the original site of Starks Tobacconist and Newsagent, a long established family business.

Caledonia Road connects Saltcoats and Ardrossan. In this 1904 view the Plantation wall has not yet been built.

Argyll Road, Saltcoats.

Looking west along Argyll Road. On the right is the Provost's lamp, the top of which is now in the North Ayrshire Museum. The young trees, once an attractive feature of Argyll and Caledonia Roads, have since been removed for reasons of safety due to the increase in traffic here.

The Mission Coast Home in Nineyards Street was founded by James Smith, a Glasgow missionary and William Bryden, Saltcoats clothier. However, it was Thomas Corbett, a merchant from the Gorbals, who actually financed the project. Opened in 1866, it was mainly used as a convalescent home for the Glasgow poor, and operates as Adelaide College of Religious Studies today.

Saltcoats' War Memorial was unveiled and dedicated on 22nd May 1922 and can be seen here in its original design of a memorial garden. The soldier's bayonet has been missing for many years. In the background is the North Parish Church. Erected in 1836 to serve the town's Gaelic speaking population, it was later used as the Ardrossan Parish Church Hall before being demolished in the seventies.

Golf Club House and Course, Saltcoats

Ardrossan and Saltcoats Golf Club was founded in 1910 and was a popular eighteen hole course until after World War II. At that time some of the ground was purchased for council housing, while the remainder became playing fields. The old golf club house, pictured here, served as the original changing rooms at Laighdykes Playing Fields, but has subsequently been demolished and replaced by a purpose built unit on Jacks Road.

Photo R.V. Brown   Saltcoats Victoria, Scottish Junior Cup Winners, 1924-5

Saltcoats' Victoria football team won the Scottish Junior Cup in the 1924-25 season, defeating St Anthony's 2-1 in the third match after drawing the first two. The local heroes and committee of the time were photographed by R.V. Brown.

L-R back row: M. Barr; Mundy; Thompson; McGinn; McMinn; Berryman; J. McLelland; McDonald; C. Nicol.

L-R front row: W. Duff; T. Keegans; O'Donnell; W. McLelland; McKenzie; W. Rainey (trainer).

AYRSHIRE Nᵒ6. (SALTCOATS) TROOP BOY SCOUTS. 1909.   PHOTO A.BROWN.

Saltcoats had two scout troops registered with the Ayrshire Scout Association, Troop no.6 under Scoutmaster John Campbell, and the 18th under W.D. Kerr. Thomas Scott, the saddler of Clytus House, stocked uniforms and equipment, and it was not unusual to be able to purchase original scout badges from his shop as late as the forties. Today Saltcoats scout troop, no.52, have their headquarters in Jacks Road.

The Burgh of Saltcoats Fire Brigade team with their handcart, 1901. Pictured left to right are J. Glen (Deputy Firemaster); C. Wallace; J. Middleton; T. Crawford; T. Millar; D. Robertson (Burgh Surveyor and Firemaster); H. Finlayson.

The North Ayrshire Museum is housed in the former Ardrossan Parish Church at the Kirkgate, built in 1744. On completion of the new Parish Church of St. Cuthbert's in 1908, the building ceased to be used as a church, and opened as a private museum in 1957. After the reorganization of local government in 1972, the newly created Cunninghame District Council assumed responsibility for local history collections such as this one, which had been gathered and cared for by the late Owen Kelly, the museum's curator and main benefactor.

Right: This interior view of the old Ardrossan Parish Church shows a model of the frigate Caledonia, suspended from a ceiling rose designed as a compass. The model was built by William Dunlop, a gunner's mate reputed to have been one of Nelson's crew at the battle of Cape St Vincent in 1797. As the story goes, Dunlop was captured by the French and built the model while in prison. He donated it to the church in 1804, and it can still be seen today in the Parish Church of St. Cuthbert, South Beach.

Brig Clytus of Saltcoats. Captain Betsy Miller in a strong North-West gale receiving her Pilot close under Houth-Head. Bound for Dublin, 13th May, 1856.

The brig Clytus was perhaps the best known of the ships that sailed between Saltcoats and Ireland, carrying coal on their outward journeys and bringing back limestone. The Clytus was particularly well known as its master was one Betsy Miller, captain of the brig from 1847 until her retirement in 1862 at seventy years of age. Betsy Miller died in 1864 and is buried in the old Kirkyard at Saltcoats.

As with many other seaside resorts, visitors came to Saltcoats for health as well as holidays. The mineral well, housed in this small building, was in the Holm Plantation and a draft of its naturally occurring spring water could be had for a penny. It was claimed that the water could cure indigestion and rheumatism, among other things, and no holiday to the town was complete without a visit to the 'physic well'. However, medical fashions changed, people lost interest in mineral cures and during the thirties the well ceased to operate. Today, no trace of either the spring or building can be found, although the amount of water often surrounding this area of the Plantation makes one wonder whether the old 'physic' still operates on occasions!

THE MINERS' HOME, SALTCOATS. 991

After World War II the National Miner's Convalescent Home in Canal Street was converted into the Maple Leaf Hotel. Later it became another hotel, the Silver Sands, and in 1989 it became a private nursing home. In 1939 a train on the old Caley Line to Ardrossan Montgomery Pier was derailed above the Miner's Home, with the death of four people. The engine landed in the grounds of the home.

45

The Saltcoats Roller Skating Rink in Glencairn Street, 1910. The main skating area had a maple wood floor, and there was a spectators gallery, a gallery for the band, and a tearoom. The rink could accommodate two hundred skaters, with electric light providing brilliant illumination at night! Several evenings during the week, the building was used as a 'picturedrome', giving what were described as 'grand moving picture performances'.

Driving Excursions.

— HAMILTON STREET. —
— SALTCOATS.—

Seamill.

Distances.

To Seamill, ...	about	6	miles
To Portincross, ...	"	8½	"
To Fairlie, ...	"	12	"
To Largs, ...	"	14	"
Round Drive to Munnoch (there and back), ...	"	17	"
Through Eglinton Policies (there and back), ...	"	16	"
To Dundonald, ...	"	13½	"
To Troon, ...	"	14	"
To Ayr, ...	"	19	"
Round Eglinton Policies (there and back) ...	"	18	"

A splendid view is obtained of the Firth of Clyde, with Arran, Bute, and Cumbraes, etc. The village of West Kilbride is approached from Seamill by road ascending the hill to the right. Visitors are recommended to drive through the village to the railway station.

James Murray, local carriage hirer, operated from the Station and Crown Hotels in Saltcoats. He had a wide variety of up to date carriages for hire including rubber tyred Landaus, Broughams, Victorias and Governess Cars. His Charabancs ran daily sightseeing tours during the summer months at very reasonable rates!

I am just off to my hotel at SALTCOATS.

Despite the cartoon on the front of this card, the writer insists he is having a good time in Saltcoats!

The Post Card Depot.

Visitors should call at
11 Dockhead Street
for

The Finest Show of High-Class Pictorial Post Cards in the district.

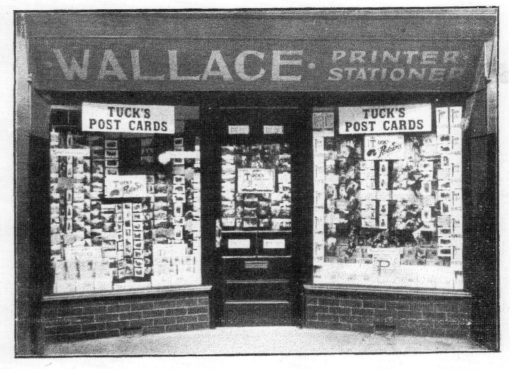

A. WALLACE, 11 Dockhead Street.

Postcard collecting was a popular hobby during Edwardian times, and the craze for cards lasted until the end of World War II. The display in A. Wallace's Dockhead Street Shop illustrates the enormous range of postcards available at the time.

Dockhead Street, Saltcoats, Nov. 5, 1926   R. V. Brown, Saltcoats

A view of Dockhead Street during the floods of November 1926. More recently, in 1991, the street flooded again with water reaching a height of four feet in some of the shops, causing widespread damage.

During the 1926 disaster the Salvation Army provided food and shelter for flood victims at their Manse Street hall.

A turn of the century view of Dockhead Street. The printing and stationery shop on the right was unique in that the parish dividing line ran at an angle through the premises and the proprietor, Mr. Wallace, had to pay his dues in part to both Ardrossan and Stevenston Parishes.